SUPER-AWESOME SCIENCE

THE SCIENCE OF
MOVIES

by Cecilia Pinto McCarthy

Content Consultant
Jocelyn Szczepaniak-Gillece
Assistant Professor of English and Film Studies
University of Wisconsin-Milwaukee

Core Library

An Imprint of Abdo Publishing
abdopublishing.com

abdopublishing.com

Published by Abdo Publishing, a division of ABDO, PO Box 398166, Minneapolis, Minnesota 55439. Copyright © 2017 by Abdo Consulting Group, Inc. International copyrights reserved in all countries. No part of this book may be reproduced in any form without written permission from the publisher. Core Library™ is a trademark and logo of Abdo Publishing.

Printed in the United States of America, North Mankato, Minnesota
042016
092016

Cover Photo: Jens Kalaene/Picture-Alliance/DPA/AP Images
Interior Photos: Jens Kalaene/Picture-Alliance/DPA/AP Images, 1; Jay Maidment/© Walt Disney Studios Motion Pictures/Everett Collection, 4; © Warner Bros. Pictures/Everett Collection, 6, 43; Glasshouse Images/Newscom, 10; Paul Moseley/MCT/Newscom, 12; Linden Artists/DK Images, 15; akg-images/Newscom, 18; Michelle Robek/Dreamstime, 21; Tony Bock/ZumaPress/Newscom, 22; Twentieth Century Fox Film Corporation/Photofest, 26; Universal Pictures/Photofest, 28, 45; Everett Collection, 31; Walt Disney Studios Motion Pictures/Photofest, 34; Walt Disney Pictures/Photofest, 37; Jeff Chiu/AP Images, 39; New Line Cinema/ Everett Collection, 41

Editor: Jon Westmark
Series Designer: Jake Nordby

Publisher's Cataloging in Publication Data
Names: McCarthy, Cecilia Pinto, author.
Title: The science of movies / by Cecilia Pinto McCarthy.
Description: Minneapolis, MN : Abdo Publishing, [2017] | Series: Super-awesome
      science | Includes bibliographical references and index.
Identifiers: LCCN 2015960501 | ISBN 9781680782479 (lib. bdg.) |
      ISBN 9781680776584 (ebook)
Subjects: LCSH: Motion pictures--Juvenile literature. | Cinematography--Juvenile
      literature.
Classification: DDC 791.43--dc23
LC record available at http://lccn.loc.gov/2015960501

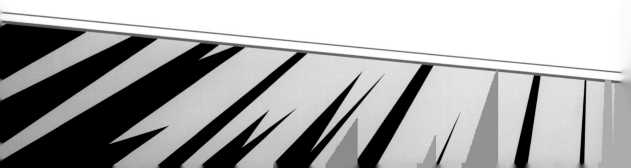

CONTENTS

CHAPTER ONE

A GRAND ILLUSION

The boom microphone swings over the set, just above the camera lens. The camera is filming an actor dressed in futuristic clothing. The actor runs across the set and leaps into the air. He is attached to wires hanging from the studio's ceiling. The wires lift him up, prolonging his hang time. A blue screen covers the wall behind him. Later a rocky, otherworldly background will be added to the scene.

Filmmakers use many different tricks to make the unbelievable come to life on screen.

The Lego Movie used computer graphics to make it appear as though everything in the film were made of toy building blocks.

Today's movies are filled with fanciful characters and heart-stopping action scenes. There are magical monsters, flying wizards, and talking toys. Creating movies is a complicated process. It can take years to complete a full-length feature film. Movie production is more than simply recording with a camera and microphone. It takes human creativity and lots of technology to make the magical world of movies.

Moving Pictures

The eyes and brain work together to produce what a person sees. The eyes take in information that is then sent to and interpreted by the brain. Sometimes what people think they see is not what is really there. This is an optical illusion.

A movie is a series of still pictures. But when we watch movies, we see motion. Two optical illusions make this possible. First when we see a picture, the image stays in our brains for a short time, even after the image is taken away. This is called persistence of vision. It helps keep the world from going dark when we blink. It also gives movies time to change the picture on the screen without us noticing. The second illusion also helps us connect the pictures on-screen. When we see a series of pictures, our brains do not notice each and every one. They connect the images. Our brains interpret changes between the pictures as motion. This illusion is called the phi phenomenon.

Early Inventions

For centuries people wanted to make still pictures move. In the 1800s, inventors made moving pictures with optical toys. One such toy is the thaumatrope. It uses a disc or card with a different picture drawn on each side. A piece of string attaches to each side of the disc. When the strings twist, the disc flips. When the disc spins quickly, the two pictures appear as one.

Optical toys were just the beginning. Several inventors improved the methods and machines for photography and film projection. One inventor was photographer Eadweard Muybridge. He was hired to answer a question: When a horse gallops, does it ever have all four hooves off the ground? It was impossible to tell by watching a horse. It ran too fast. But Muybridge had an idea. He set up cameras along a racetrack. Each camera had a wire that ran across the track. As the horse ran, it tripped the wires. One by one the cameras took pictures. The photos proved that indeed there was a moment when the horse had all its hooves off the ground. In 1879 Muybridge unveiled a new projector. He called it the zoopraxiscope. The device projected light through a glass disc as it spun. Muybridge put the images of the trotting horse onto a disc. As it spun, the images appeared to move.

In 1887 an American minister named Hannibal Goodwin developed a flexible film. It was made from a plastic material called celluloid. The celluloid was coated with light-sensitive chemicals. The see-through film could be rolled on to a spool. People started developing machines that used celluloid film.

Flammable Film

Until the 1950s, celluloid film was made with flammable ingredients. Its main chemical, cellulose nitrate, was originally used as an explosive. As the film ran through a projector, it sometimes ignited from the heat of hot lightbulbs. Aging film kept in canisters also became a problem. When the film breaks down, it gives off gases. Gases built up in a canister can cause a fire if they get too warm. Nitrate-based films are safely stored and preserved by keeping them in cold storage.

An operator turned a handle on the Cinématographe to change the images that appeared on screen.

The machines used the film to record and project moving images.

In 1895 French brothers Louis and Auguste Lumìere demonstrated one of the earliest movie projectors. They called their invention the Cinématographe. It was a projector, camera, and printer all in one. The Cinématographe was small. Now movies could be shot almost anywhere. On December 28, 1895, the Lumìere brothers projected ten short black-and-white films. It was the first time that movies played on screen for a paying audience.

In 1913 inventor Thomas Edison was interviewed about the future of the movie industry. When asked about the value of movies to education, he stated:

> *Books will soon be obsolete in the public schools. Scholars will be instructed through the eye. It is possible to teach every branch of human knowledge with the motion picture. Our school system will be completely changed inside of ten years. We have been working for some time on the school pictures. We have been studying and reproducing the life of the fly, mosquito, silk weaving moth, . . . and various other insects. . . . It proves conclusively the worth of motion pictures in chemistry, physics, and other branches of study, making the scientific truths, difficult to understand from text books, plain and clear to children.*

Source: Frederick James Smith. *"The Evolution of the Motion Picture, VI: Looking Into the Future With Thomas A. Edison."* The New York Dramatic Mirror *July 9, 1913: 24.* Print.

Back It Up

In this passage, Thomas Edison uses evidence to support a main point. Write a paragraph describing the point he is making. What evidence does Edison use to support his point?

CHAPTER TWO

CAPTURED ON CAMERA

At its most basic level, moviemaking is recording sights and sounds. Over the years, one of the biggest changes has been in camera technology. Analog cameras record images directly onto film. The recorded images represent the actual scene. Digital cameras work differently. They convert images into numbers. These numbers can then be stored or translated into images on a screen.

Filmmakers use many devices to get the right camera angle. Jibs are long arms that allow filmmakers to film high or low.

Film Movie Cameras

Film used for recording movies comes in different gauges, or widths. The most common width is 35 millimeters. The film reel is loaded into a camera, which works much like the human eye. The front of the camera holds a lens. As a scene is filmed, light enters through the lens. Next the light is split into two beams. One beam passes down to the eyepiece. The camera operator can see what is being filmed. The other beam of light passes through the shutter. The shutter is a disk that opens and closes. When the film is exposed to light, chemicals on its surface change.

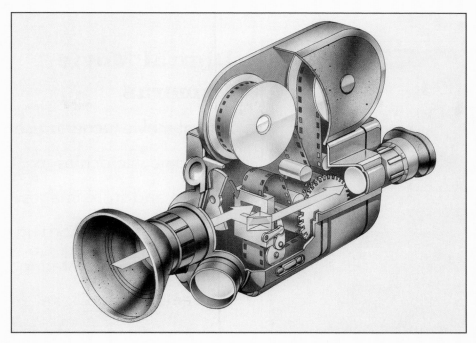

Shooting with Analog

There are many parts inside a film movie camera. Look at this diagram of a camera. The yellow arrow represents the direction light takes. The red arrow indicates the spinning of the shutter. Where does the light hit the film?

Shutters are often set to turn 24 times per second. This is called the frame rate. In between frames, the shutter blocks light. This gives the next frame time to move into place. Later the film goes through a chemical process in a lab. Chemicals develop the images on the film. After it dries, the film is ready to be printed and shown.

Digital versus Film

Although digital filmmaking has been around for years, many filmmakers still use 35-millimeter film. Some film professionals think movies made with digital equipment lack the warmth, texture, and color of film movies. Others choose to record with digital cameras. Digital can be easier to edit, store, and ship. And most theatres now use digital projectors. Directors do not always choose one format over the other. Director J. J. Abrams shot the 2015 movie *Star Wars: The Force Awakens* on film and later converted it to digital to include three-dimensional effects.

Digital Movie Cameras

Digital movie cameras use electronic microchips to capture and store images. Like film, digital recording begins with light entering the camera lens. Digital cameras use sensors to detect incoming light and convert it into electrical signals. Then the signals are stored digitally as strings of ones and zeros. This method allows huge amounts of data to be stored on small electronic chips.

Writer and director Colin Trevorrow has made movies using both film and digital cameras. He explained how he views choosing between the two during a discussion at the Sundance Film Festival in 2016:

> In the end, these are all artistic choices, and they're creative choices, and I feel what is most important to me about film is that people have the choice to use it. It's not that I would say one should do this or one should do the other. You don't go to the symphony to hear the [best violin]. You go to hear the violinist. And the violinist is going to choose the best possible violin—of course they will. I choose to make films with the best possible violin.

Source: Ross A. Lincoln. "Power of Story: The Art of Film with Christopher Nolan, Colin Trevorrow, and Rachel Morrison." Indiewire.com. Indiewire, January 29, 2016. Web. March 15, 2016.

What's the Big Idea?

Read the passage carefully. How does Trevorrow use the symphony to talk about making movies? What does Trevorrow's comparison say about how he views film?

FROM SILENCE TO SOUND

The first movies were silent. There was no dialogue or other sound. Many theaters filled in the missing sounds. Sometimes actors added dialogue from behind the screen. Other times live musicians played music in the movie theater.

In the mid-1920s, the Vitaphone was introduced. The Vitaphone recorded the sounds of actors as they acted. The record played while the movie was shown.

Many silent films had musical scores that accompanied the action of the film.

But the Vitaphone system had many problems. Once the record was made, no sounds could be changed. Sometimes the sounds did not match the action on the screen. Worst of all, the wax records wore out after just 20 plays.

Analog Sound-on-Film

Between 1920 and 1930, inventors Lee DeForest and Theodore Case came up with a way to use light to record sound right onto a strip of film.

In sound-on-film, first a microphone picks up sound waves. The sound waves are then turned into electric current. The current controls a light that shines on the film. As the sound signals change, the brightness of the light changes too. The changes in light intensity are recorded on the sound filmstrip. When the film is played, another light shines through the film. A receiver picks up the changes in the light beam. The receiver turns the light signals into electric signals. The electric signals get played as sound through a loudspeaker.

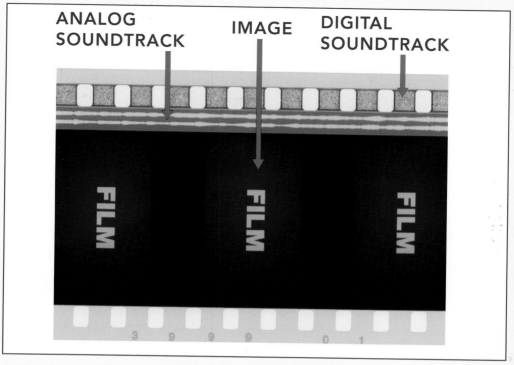

Sound-on-Film

Many filmstrips contain both analog and digital soundtracks. The diagram above shows where images and sounds are stored on a filmstrip. From what you've read, what is the benefit of having the sound and images on one filmstrip?

Digital Sound-on-Film

Instead of turning sound information into light signals, digital recording turns sound into a series of numbers. The numbers are printed as a sound code onto the edge of the filmstrip. To play back the sounds, the film is put through a reader on a film projector. The reader converts the digital code back into sound.

Sound artists use many different tools to create sound effects.

Sound Production

Sound is a big part of the movie experience. It helps tell the story. It sets the mood as the movie scenes change. Movies contain many layers of sounds. Actors speak while music plays in the background of a scene. Fast, loud music adds a sense of excitement and action. Soft, slow music can make the viewer feel calm, sad, or scared. Sound effects, such as howling wind and zooming traffic, add an immersive touch. Movie sounds are added during different parts of the moviemaking process. Some are recorded on location during filming. Other sounds are added in later during the postproduction process.

Dialogue is usually recorded on location as the action takes place. Some background noises are also recorded. Several types of microphones are used. Microphones pick up sound vibrations. They change the sounds

Surround Sound

Today's movie theaters use digital surround sound systems. The systems project sound into the theater from many angles. During the production process, different movie sounds are recorded separately. When the movie plays in the theater, the sounds are channeled to speakers placed all around the room. The audience hears sounds coming from all directions. Dialogue may come from speakers near the screen. Other sounds like traffic rumbling in the background may come from speakers placed toward the back of the theater. Surround sound systems also move sounds around the theater to match how action moves on screen.

Foley Artists

While shooting on location, directors focus on the actors, the action, and recording dialogue. Capturing background sounds is not as important. During the postproduction process, Foley artists add sounds to movies to create a more complete experience. Foley artists get their name from Jack Foley, a sound editor who developed many ways for making sound effects. Sometimes Foley artists must be extra creative. They use everyday objects to mimic sounds. For instance, the sound of Spider-Man's shooting webs in the 2002 *Spider-Man* movie was made when a Foley artist strummed fishing line.

into electrical signals. The signals are then recorded.

Some microphones are attached to long poles called booms. Boom microphones help capture speech without getting in the way. Covers over the microphones keep out unwanted noises. Lavalier microphones are a type of miniature microphone. They are easy to hide. "Lavs" can be clipped under an actor's hair or under a collar. They also might be hidden in nearby scenery or attached to props.

A great number of movie sounds are added after the film has been shot. Sound editors and movie directors review the recorded film. They make a list of sounds that must be changed or added. A team of sound experts fixes the problems with the dialogue, and they also add sound effects. They use recording devices and machines called mixers. Mixers process the different sounds that have been recorded. They can balance sounds and change sound volumes. The team can choose which sounds to keep and which to get rid of.

EXPLORE ONLINE

Chapter Three discusses sound technology. The website below discusses how science and technology help blind and deaf people enjoy the movie experience. How is the information from the website the same as the information in Chapter Three? What new information did you learn from the website?

Caption Devices
mycorelibrary.com/science-of-movies

CHAPTER FOUR

SPECIAL EFFECTS AND MOVIE MAGIC

Special effects are illusions or tricks that make the impossible seem real on screen. Special effects are created using makeup, props, and computer images. Maybe a scene calls for an explosion or an alien creature. Special effects can do the job. Special effects can be mechanical or optical. Science makes both mechanical and optical effects possible.

Some acting roles require hours of hair and makeup preparation.

Although safety harnesses and wires can be edited out digitally, some actors must still perform difficult stunts.

Mechanical Effects

Mechanical special effects are those that are physical. Stunts, props, scenery, models, makeup, and pyrotechnics are all mechanical effects. Mechanical effects are used while a movie is being filmed.

Stunts add action and excitement to movies. A stunt is an action that requires special skill. Cars fly over ramps and trains dangle from bridges. Actors perform acrobatic feats. Stunts can be difficult and dangerous. Movie directors often work with physicists and engineers to ensure stunts are safe to do.

Movie special effects teams build models of buildings and other large structures. Models are easier to build than full-scale buildings. Miniature models are filmed close to the camera lens. This tricks the viewer by changing the perspective. The models appear much larger than they really are. The castle from the Harry Potter films is actually a model. It is only 50 feet (15 m) wide.

Sometimes a movie calls for pyrotechnics such as a fire or explosion. Miniature models take the place of the real thing. It is easier, cheaper, and less dangerous to blow up a model.

Animatronics

Animatronic machines are mechanical puppets similar to robots. They can be preprogrammed or moved using remote control. Animatronics fill in for wild animals or creatures such as monsters or dinosaurs. Engineers who build animatronics are skilled in mechanics, electricity, and computer science. Famous animatronic movie creatures include the shark in *Jaws*, E. T. the alien, and the *Apatosaurus* in *Jurassic World*.

On-screen fires and explosions are caused by chemical reactions. Experts know the proper way to use gases, explosives, and chemicals. They carefully measure amounts to control the reactions. Adding special chemicals makes flames and explosions brighter and more colorful.

Chemicals are necessary to create makeup such as fake blood and alien skin. Latex and silicone are two popular materials in special effects departments. They can be molded into masks and body parts. There are even recipes for fake glass. Sugar glass replaces real glass so that actors do not get hurt. It was originally made by mixing sugar, water, corn syrup, and another chemical. Now fake glass is molded from a type of plastic called resin.

Chemicals are also an important part of recreating weather on screen. Fog and snow are made with chemical reactions. For example, mixing dry ice and hot water produces a thick fog. Snow is made from torn paper. The paper must be torn or else it doesn't

Fake glass helps actors perform stunts that involve breaking glass without getting hurt.

fall like real snow. Fake snow is also made from a chemical called a polymer. The snow polymer is similar to the polymer that absorbs wetness in baby diapers.

Optical Effects

Optical effects take place during and after filming. One of the oldest and simplest forms of optical effect is double exposure. A scene is filmed, and then the film is rewound. Next a different scene is filmed over the first. Objects from the second scene then appear transparent in the first.

Mattes also help create visual tricks. Mattes are background paintings. Often part of the painting is blacked out. When filmed, the black parts of the matte do not expose the film to light. Those parts of the film can be filmed again with real people or objects. Mattes allow artists to put real actors into imaginary scenes.

Today's movies use a special effect technique called chroma-key compositing. Chroma-key uses computer technology to insert any background into a scene. Actors are filmed in front of a green screen. The finished video is then run through a computer program. The program checks the colors in the video. It removes the green color and replaces it with a chosen background. Sometimes the screen used is blue instead of green. This depends on the colors of the clothing or other objects being filmed.

FURTHER EVIDENCE

Chapter Four discusses mechanical and optical effects. Read the article at the link below. It discusses how Spider-Man's stunt double makes the acrobatic moves appear real. What is the main point of the article? What new information does it provide about special effects?

The Physics of Spider-Man
mycorelibrary.com/science-of-movies

CHAPTER FIVE

AMAZING ANIMATION

Animators are artists who make art come to life. The art may be drawings or puppets. It may be made from paper, clay, or computer images. Animation is based on tricking the eye. The creators of the early optical toys were animators. They made simple drawings seem to move. Today a successful animated film relies on the skills of actors, artists, mathematicians, computer experts, and scientists.

The robot BB-8 in *Star Wars: The Force Awakens* was created using both puppets and animation.

Stop-Motion

Stop-motion animation uses objects such as puppets or clay figures as movie characters. The frames of the movie are shot one at a time. Between each shot, the object is moved a tiny bit. Then the next frame is shot. The illusion is created when the frames are joined in order. Our eyes and brain link the tiny changes together. The characters come alive with movement. Crafting top quality stop-motion animation is a lengthy process. Just one minute of film can take several months and hundreds of frames to film. The Wallace and Gromit movies are examples of stop-motion animation.

Cel

Celluloid is a clear plastic material. It is the same material used to make film. Celluloid, or cel, animation works much the same way as stop-motion animation. Artists draw or paint the background scene. The character is drawn in different positions on separate cel sheets. Each character drawing is slightly

Animators often use separate cels for their characters and backgrounds so they do not need to draw entire scenes many times.

different than the one before it. The cels are layered on top of the background scene. When photographed in a series, the characters appear to move.

As they age, cels become damaged. Today cels from Disney movies made up until 1989 are stored in a special building. There are over 200,000 cels stored

Multiplane Camera

Walt Disney was a pioneer in the field of cel animation. Over the years, his company developed many technologies that transformed animation. Disney technician Bill Garity patented the multiplane camera. The camera filmed through a series of glass shelves. Cel animations were placed on the shelves. The layers of cels could be placed closer to the camera or farther away. This made it look like the scenes had depth. In 1938 The Walt Disney Company was awarded a Scientific and Engineering Academy Award for its invention.

at the Disney Animation Research Library.

Computer-Generated Animation

The digital age changed the world of animation. There are many types of computer animation. Characters may be simple, flat images or realistic three-dimensional (3-D) beings.

Two-dimensional, or 2-D, animation is based on the basic stop-motion and cel techniques. Some 2-D animators draw each picture and transfer them to computers. Another method is to use a computer animation program to

Clay models can be combined with animation to create 3-D characters with more depth.

draw the characters and scenes. 2-D animation is used mostly in television shows. The television show *The Simpsons* is done in 2-D animation.

Computer graphics can also create what look like 3-D characters and images. Artists work with lighting, camera, set, and computer experts. First the movie idea and characters are sketched out on paper. Then a sculptor makes clay models of the characters. Computer experts study the clay models. To computerize the models, they use math concepts such as geometry. They must also be able to use many software programs. Body movements, colors, and lighting bring the characters to life. Animators consult with scientists to ensure that movements, such as splashing water and moving body parts, are realistic. Pixar Animation Studios's *Toy Story* was made with computer technology. In fact, it was the first completely computer-generated movie.

Computer-generated imagery (CGI) is not just for character design. CGI allows animators to make imaginary worlds seem real. Movies such as *Jurassic World* and *Avatar* use animated backgrounds and characters.

CGI is sometimes used with another technology known as motion capture. Motion capture technology captures the movements of a real person. Special markers are placed all over an actor's body. As the actor moves, his or her actions are captured by special cameras placed around the room. This information is sent to a computer where it is used to create a digital skeleton. Animators apply the movements to an animated character. Motion capture gives animated

Motion capture helped give Gollum in the *Lord of the Rings* films more realistic movements.

characters fluid, realistic movements. A well-known motion capture character is Gollum, the creature in the *Lord of the Rings* movies.

The Future of Movies

The future of moviemaking is bright. As people from different fields work together, new technologies and techniques will continue to develop. Science, math, technology, and art are changing the way movies are created, projected, and experienced.

FAST FACTS

- Movies take advantage of two optical illusions that make people see motion on screen.
- Analog cameras record movies on film.
- When film is exposed to light, chemicals on the film record an image of the scene.
- Digital cameras convert images into code that gets stored on microchips.
- Moviemakers use both analog and digital technologies, though many filmmakers prefer the way film records images.
- In the early years of film, sounds and music were sometimes played in the movie theater.
- Sound-on-film allows the images and sounds to match on screen.
- Sound editors and Foley artists add sounds in after movies have been filmed.
- Mechanical and optical effects help bring unrealistic parts of movies to life.

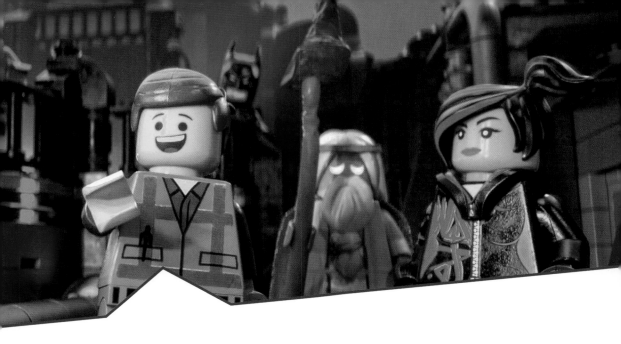

- Stop-motion animation records tiny changes in clay figures or puppets to make it appear as though they are moving.
- Cel animation uses layers of drawings to create scenes so that when something changes the whole scene does not need to be redrawn.
- Animators today use computer programs to help create movies.
- Motion capture allows animators to give their computer-generated characters realistic movements.

STOP AND THINK

Surprise Me

Chapter One discusses movies as moving pictures. After reading this chapter, what two or three facts about movie history did you find most surprising? Write a few sentences about each fact. Why did you find each fact surprising?

Tell the Tale

Chapter Four of this book discusses mechanical and optical special effects. Pretend you are making a movie. What special effects would it have? Include both mechanical and optical effects. What would you need to create the effects?

Say What?

Studying the science of movies can mean learning a lot of new vocabulary. Find five words in this book you've never heard before. Use a dictionary to find out what they mean. Then write the meanings in your own words and use each word in a new sentence.

Take a Stand

Many of today's movies use computer animation to create new scenes and characters. Some people think animated movies are better than live-action movies. Others think there is too much computer animation in today's films. What do you think?

GLOSSARY

dialogue
the things that are said by the characters in a story or movie

digital
using computer technology

microchip
tiny electronic circuits on a small piece of hard material

polymer
a chemical compound that is made of small molecules arranged in a repeating structure to form a larger molecule

postproduction
the period after filming during which the movie is prepared for final presentation

pyrotechnics
devices used to make fires and explosions

shutter
the part of a camera that opens to allow light in when a picture is taken

spool
a cylinder or roller on which film can be wound

transparent
an object or surface through which light can pass

LEARN MORE

Books

Baggaley, Ann, ed. *Children's Book of the Movies: Explore the Magical, Behind-the-Scenes World of the Movies*. New York: DK Children, 2014.

Wolf, Steve. *The Secret Science Behind Movie Stunts & Special Effects*. New York: Sky Horse, 2007.

Websites

To learn more about Super-Awesome Science, visit **booklinks.abdopublishing.com**. These links are routinely monitored and updated to provide the most current information available.

Visit **mycorelibrary.com** for free additional tools for teachers and students.

INDEX

ABOUT THE AUTHOR

Cecilia Pinto McCarthy has written several nonfiction books for children. She also teaches environmental science classes at a nature sanctuary. She and her family live north of Boston, Massachusetts.